Contents

Any words appearing in the text in bold, **like this**, are explained in the Glossary.

What is a pulley?

A machine is a man-made **device**. All machines make our lives easier by helping us to do jobs. This simple machine is called a pulley.

This woman is using a pulley to lift water from a well. It is much easier to lift the water container with the pulley than by hand.

What does a pulley do?

A pulley makes a pull in one direction into a pull in another direction. The workman is pulling down on the rope, and the rope is pulling up on the bucket.

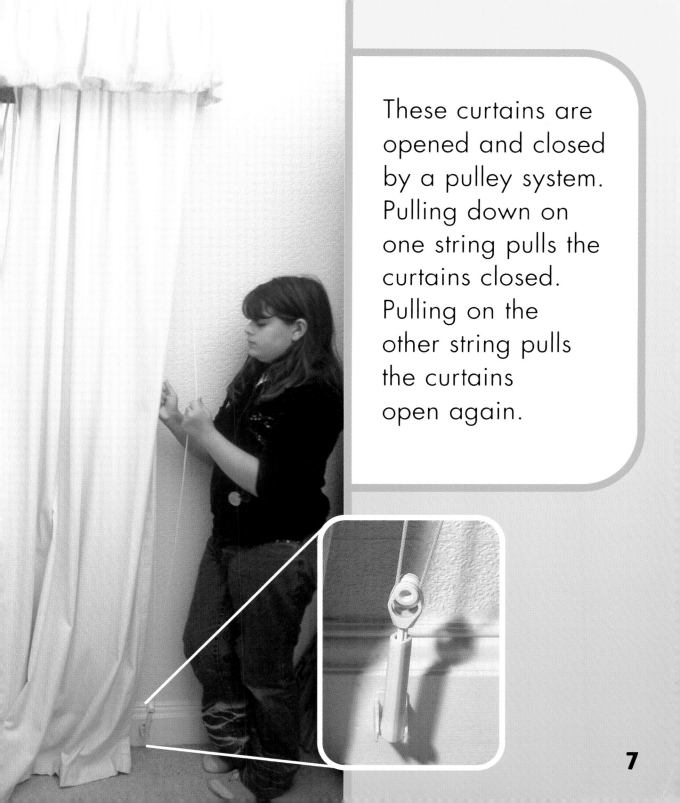

These curtains are opened and closed by a pulley system. Pulling down on one string pulls the curtains closed. Pulling on the other string pulls the curtains open again.

7

Pulley parts

wheel

A pulley has two parts. One part is a wheel with a **groove**. This is called a pulley wheel. The other part is a rope or wire that fits in the groove.

groove

rope

teeth

chain

Some pulleys have chains instead of ropes or wires. The holes in the chain fit over teeth around the pulley wheel. This stops the chain slipping as the wheel turns.

How does a pulley work?

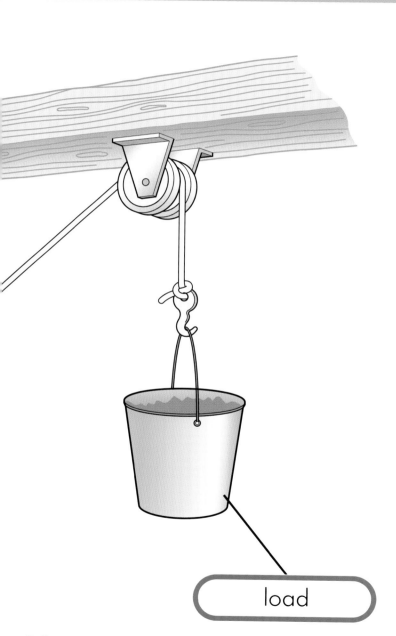

A pulley is used to lift or move a **load**. This pulley is being used to lift a bucket. The load is the weight of the bucket pulling down.

load

effort

The pull a person makes on the rope is called the **effort**. If the effort is strong enough, it becomes bigger than the load. Then the rope starts moving.

Pulleys for lifting

A pulley at the top of this pole lifts the flag upwards. The pulley makes it easy to pull the flag up because you can pull down on the rope.

pulley wheel

This tow truck has a pulley for lifting motor vehicles. A wire goes over the pulley wheel on the end of the arm, and down to a hook that lifts the vehicle.

Pulleys for pulling

This washing line goes round pulleys. After the woman has pegged the wet clothes to the washing line, she pulls the empty line to move the washing outwards above the street.

pulley

string

Here is another pulley that changes the direction of a pull. Pulling down on the string pulls the two blades of the **pruner** together. The blades slice through the branches easily.

Joining pulleys

A loop of rope or chain can be put round two pulley wheels. When one wheel turns, it makes the other wheel turn, too.

chain

On a motorbike a chain joins the engine to the back wheel. When the pulley wheel on the engine turns, it makes the back wheel turn too. This pushes the bike along.

Faster and slower

The pulley wheel on the bicycle pedals is larger than the pulley wheel on the back wheel. This makes the back wheel turn faster than the pedals.

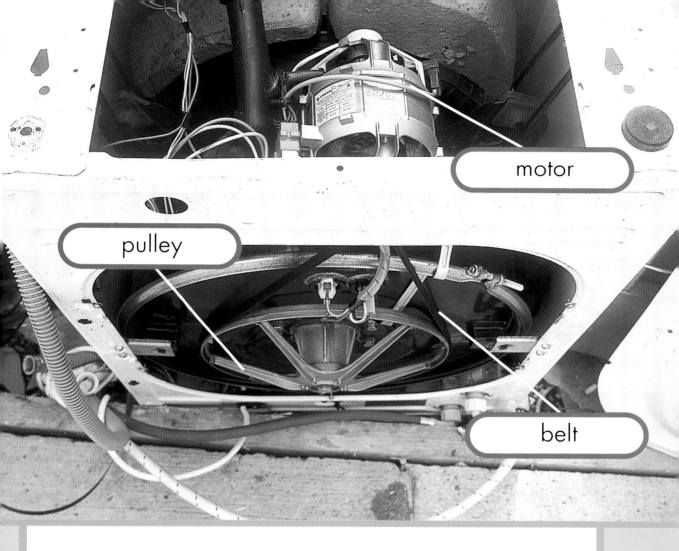

motor

pulley

belt

An **electric** motor turns the large **drum** inside a washing machine. The motor has a small pulley wheel and the drum has a large one. The motor turns faster than the drum.

Pulleys working together

blocks

A **block and tackle** is made up of pulleys working together. A rope or chain goes round all the pulleys. When the rope is pulled, the blocks move towards each other.

A block and tackle is used to lift very heavy weights, such as this sunken boat. The block and tackle makes the **effort** needed much smaller than the **load**.

Pulleys on cranes

Cranes need lots of pulleys. There are pulleys at the end of this crane's **boom**. Wires go round the pulleys and down to the hook that lifts the **load**.

hook

boom

This floating crane lifts sections of a gas production platform into place. It can lift hundreds of **tonnes**. It has a giant **block and tackle** with dozens of pulley wheels.

Pulleys on boats

Sailing boats have pulleys for raising and **adjusting** the sails, and for **steering**. The ropes that move the sails go through pulleys. Pulling a rope moves the sail.

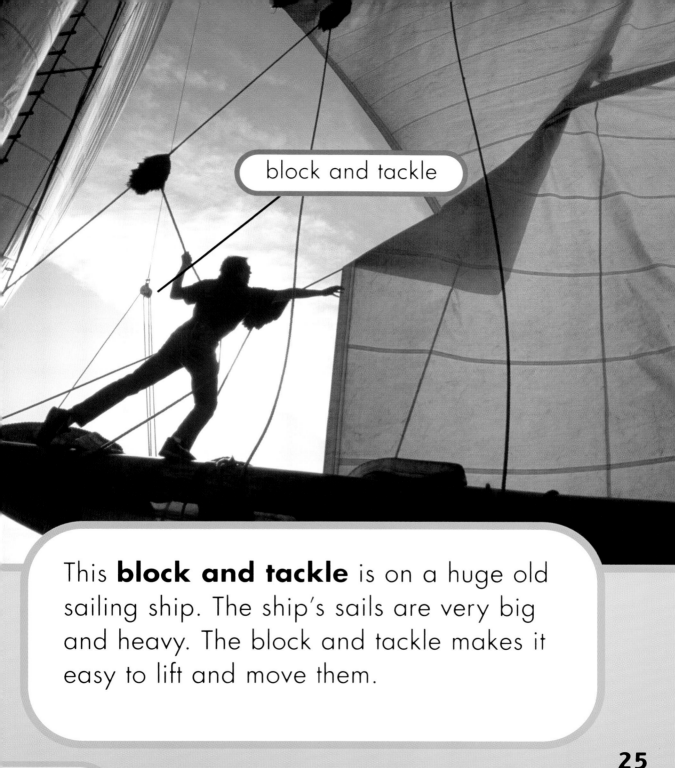

block and tackle

This **block and tackle** is on a huge old sailing ship. The ship's sails are very big and heavy. The block and tackle makes it easy to lift and move them.

Pulleys in machines

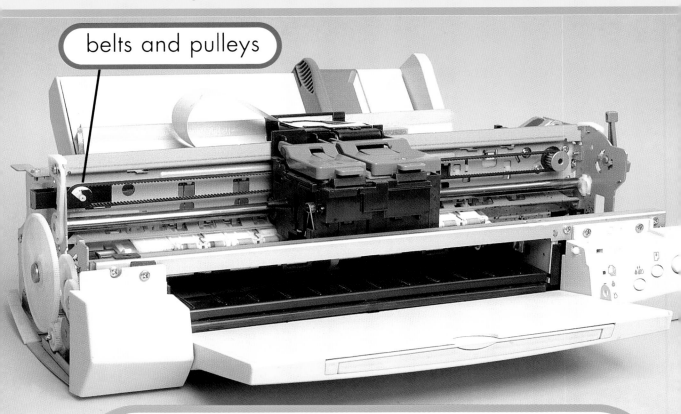

belts and pulleys

Many complicated machines have pulleys inside. This is the inside of a computer printer. The **print head** sprays the ink. The pulleys and belts make it move backwards and forwards.

In this car engine there is a belt that goes round lots of pulley wheels. The engine turns one of the pulley wheels. This makes the other pulley wheels turn too. One of pulley wheels turns a **generator** that makes **electricity** for the car.

Amazing pulley facts

- The pulley is one of the oldest machines in the world. It was invented more than 2500 years ago.
- Sailing ships were invented a long time before engines and motors. Sailors lifted and moved the heavy sails with pulleys and **blocks and tackles**.
- A lift in a building has a huge block and tackle that moves the lift car up and down the lift **shaft**.

- Street cars, like this one in San Francisco, are pulled along the hilly roads on underground cables. At the central power station there are huge pulley wheels that transfer power from **motors** to the cables.

Glossary

adjust	change slightly
block and tackle	machine made up of pulleys with a rope or chain going round all of them
boom	long lifting arm on a crane
device	thing that does a job. A clothes peg is a device. So is an electronic calculator.
drum	round container (like a tin can) in a washing machine that the clothes go inside
effort	pull on a pulley that you use to lift or move the load
electric/ electricity	power that gives us light and heat and can make machines work
generator	machine that makes electricity when it is turned round

groove	long narrow hole in an object, especially for something to fit into
load	pull on a pulley from the thing the pulley is trying to lift or move
print head	part of a printer that puts ink on to the paper
pruner	tool for cutting branches
shaft	spinning rod
steer	make a vehicle or a boat change direction
tonne	measure of weight. A small car weighs about one tonne.

More books to read

Pulleys and Gears, Angela Royston (Heinemann Library, 2000)

What Do Pulleys and Gears Do?, David Glover (Heinemann Library, 1996)

Pulleys, Michael Dahl (Franklin Watts, 2000)

Toybox Science: Gears, Chris Ollerenshaw and Pat Triggs (A and C Black, 2001)

Index